Lessons and Blessings

TINISA HUFF

BookLeaf Publishing

Presentation by *BookLeaf Publishing*

Web: www.bookleafpub.com

E-mail: info@bookleafpub.com

ISBN: 9789358366655

First edition 2023

INDEX

BLACK GIRL MAGIC

(dedicated to all the strong black women I know who are black girls who rock)

We all have that special fire inside
you know that pride
THAT BLACK GIRL MAGIC

We got that strength, that courage, that joy
you know the difference between a girl and a boy
it makes us stand out
It's what THEY want to be about
THAT BLACK GIRL MAGIC

It's our culture, our hair
the stylish clothes we wear
It's the way we walk, the way we speak
our bodies have the brothas weak
THAT BLACK GIRL MAGIC

It's the way we demand respect
even though we are flawed and far from perfect
It's the way we continue to shine
Because we believe in excellence and stay on the grind
THAT BLACK GIRL MAGIC

We exude GREATNESS
We are POWERFUL and COURAGEOUS
We possess BEAUTY and GRACE
We are the face
of adversity and triumph
We are often imitated but never duplicated
Because we have that BLACK GIRL MAGIC

GRANDMA'S LOVE

Grandma's love is cooking chicken and dumplings, salmon
croquettes and dressing
Grandma's love is oiling your scalp and combing your hair
Grandma's love is washing clothes and hemming a dress because
you can't
Grandma's love is taking you to birthday parties
and making sure you ride in the first seat on the first car of the EL
Grandma's love is the stories and lessons she shares
Grandma's love is the memories she makes with her grandchildren

Grandma's love is never-ending
Grandma's love is forgiving
Grandma's love is comforting
There is no love like a grandmother's love
She will love you unconditionally
She will love you with her soul
Her love transforms you
Her love teaches you
Her love lives inside you
Without her love you will be incomplete
A grandmother's love is God's blessing

LOVE IS...

Love is...
early mornings and late nights
kisses and holding me tight

Love is...
understanding and making mistakes
doing whatever it takes to put a smile on each other's face

Love is...
remembering the little things that mean the most
sharing your dreams, your fears, your hopes

Love is...
Good morning beautiful texts
and I miss you phone calls
being vulnerable and breaking down walls

Love is...
laughter, a vibe, chemistry
an indescribable feeling that energy
between two people
who are perfectly imperfect
with flaws and all
but still....Love each other

AND THEN YOU CAME

Out of nowhere you appeared

and erased all my fears

about love and being loved

God must have sent you from above

I stopped looking and you found me

erasing all my doubts and insecurities

feeding my mind and my soul

teaching me things to make me whole

guiding me and leading me along the way

promising me that your love is here to stay

who would have ever thought I'd meet you

that you would bring so much joy to my world

that you'd want to make me your girl

your wife, your partner for life

we laugh and we talk you're like my best friend

I pray that this feeling never ends

and although we've only been in each other's lives for a short time

I know that I belong to you and you are mine

It's just a matter of time before we make it official

you are an original, a one-of-a kind man

mr protector, a leader, a teacher

I'll do everything in my power to keep ya

because I need you and you need me

this is fate....our destiny
and nothing will break us apart
you already have my heart
I know I'll never be the same
because of the day you came

EDUCATED THUG

What I need in my life is a thug
But not any type of thug, an educated thug
The type of brotha who is smart and in control
But won't sell his soul
To some drug dealer or jail cell
See he keeps his shit on lock
Even though he might have been around the block
He graduated from high school and went to college
And gained more knowledge on how to really treat a woman
He opens doors and pulls out chairs
Tells her she's beautiful and loves the smell of her hair
He's not afraid to show his sensitive side
He's a real nigga he doesn't care about his pride
He's not standing on a street corner
He's working nine to five
He's not thinking about hustlin cuz his woman's by his side

I need a thug in my life
An educated thug, a god-fearing man,
A strong black man
Who knows that the world is in his hands
But, first he has to stop blaming the white man
He has to get up off his ass and get his

Own job and his own crib, make his own money so that he can live
And be strong for the black woman
Who needs him to hold her to love her to comfort her
To support her no matter what she does
That's an educated thug
He's not slangin' rocks or doggin' gunshots
He's not drinking forties and hangin' with his homies
Or getting some chick pregnant that he banged last night
He wants a real relationship a family and a wife
He's not satisfied with making 40,000 a year
He wants to make six figures and have a real career
He votes and speaks his mind
Knows how to unwind and have a good time
He'll knock another nigga out if he has to
He'll never let another nigga disrespect him or his boo
He loves making his woman happy
Don't give a shit if her hair is weaved out or nappy
Just as long as he can see her smile

I want an educated thug
A brotha that can handle all of me
My mind, soul and spirituality
So if you know or see an educated thug
Tell him to come holla at a sista and show me some love.

SAD LOVE SONG

How many times are we gonna hear the same sad love song
you know the one about the man who always does the woman wrong
lying to her, cheating on her, he ain't neva got the time
except when he wants to bump n' grind and hit it from behind
tells her the stuff he thinks she wants to hear
knowing all along that a relationship is his biggest fear

what about the sad love song when a woman gives her heart to a man
just to see him stand
at the end of an aisle beside another woman
leaving her to feel used, abused and confused
now she gotta pick her face up off the ground
turn her life around
and try to trust and believe in another man

or how about the sad love song where the woman takes care of
the man
and he can't even put 10 dollars in her hand
she works all day, takes care of her home
while he sits and plays video games and uses her phone
he's got big hopes and big dreams
but can never keep a job it seems

when are we gonna stop singing these sad love songs
when are we gonna tell these trifiin' negroes
to get gone and leave us alone
we have to stop using our bodies
as a temporary tool
to get some fool to love us
there's no trust in a night of lust
we have to start loving with our heads and not with our hearts
if we want a fresh start
and a real shot at happiness
without all the drama and stress
that we go through in some relationships

I want to sing a love song that makes me feel so good inside
like I'm on a rollercoaster ride or high
off some powerful drug
these sad love songs don't do shit but give me the blues
hell I'm tired of feeling used
I want to sing a love song that makes me feel warm
and keeps me safe from harm
a song that makes me cry happy tears
and takes away all of my fears
a song that will love me for me
and not what they think I should be

can somebody call the radio stations and tell them to please
stop playing these sad love songs
I need to hear some happy songs so I can move on.

I USED TO LOVE HIM

I used to love him, but he didn't love me, you see
He left me for a woman who was less opinionated and had a big ass
who lacked education and class, but continued to let him smash
without putting a ring on it

I used to love him, but he didn't love me, you see
because I refused to be used and when I wouldn't let him drive my car
He said, "baby, you've gone too far",
and when I wouldn't pay his phone bill
He said "baby, for real".
He laughed and I said, "ain't nobody got time for dat".

I used to love him, but he didn't love me, you see
He refused to commit and was doing illegal ish
He wanted to party all night and sleep all day
when the bill came at dinner and it was time to pay
He politely turned his head and pushed the check my way

I used to love him, but he didn't love me, you see
He never spent HIS money we always went somewhere free
He didn't wine and dine, would only give me a few minutes of his time
before he was on to the next thing
even though he claimed I made his soul sing

I used to love him, but he didn't love me, you see
I realized that I'm the prize and he needs to recognize the
woman that I am
I used to love him, but he didn't love me, you see
I learned you can't change a man
and after you've done all you can you stand
Up and walk away and wait for God to send you a man that will
love you the way you... Used....to... Love... Him

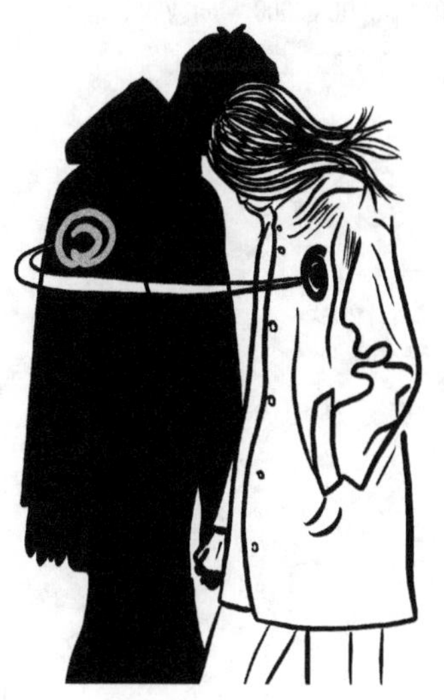

LET GO

When the body gets weary, you just have to let go

When your soul needs a rest, you just have to let go

When you know that you have done all that you can, you just

have to let go

No more pain, no more sickness, no more worry

Because you have let go

God wants us to let go

But keep the memories they will help soothe your pain

Know that there will be peace when you let go

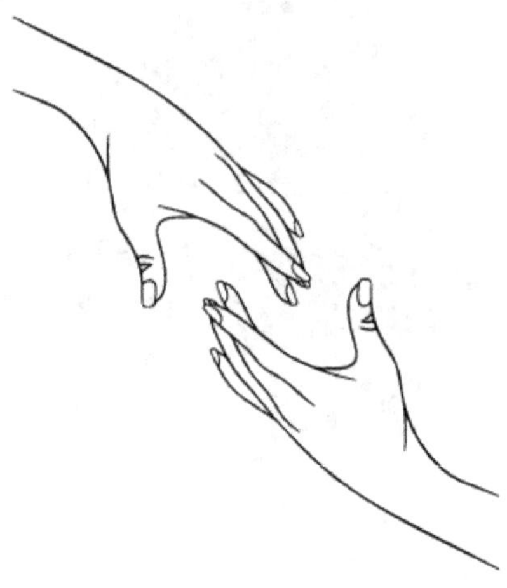

THE EPITOME OF A BLACK WOMAN

She is the epitome of a black woman

Her poise, her grace

the youth upon her face

A voice as loud as the music that she loves

A born leader an educated diva

She's a bad mamma jamma

a brickhouse from way back in the day

dancing the night away

Stepping and sliding with her cool moves,

cool style and cool attitude

She is irreplaceable, unforgettable and remarkable

A phenomenal woman a Nubian queen

with great determination

an inspiration to her family, a role model for her community

she has a warm heart an entertaining home

she's not afraid of who she is

she knows exactly where she belongs

with the energy of a teenager,

but the knowledge of a wise woman

carrying strength within her hands

and love within her heart

she does her best from the beginning to the end

to you she may be a true and everlasting friend,

but to me she is my mother.

FLOW

Ever feel like you are just waiting....

for something great to happen

for the storm to pass

to be happy

to be healthier

to be richer

to do all of the things you love

for a sign to take the next step

for a leap of faith

for permission to be yourself

for life to go the way you planned

but then, you realize God is in control

so you just have to go with the flow

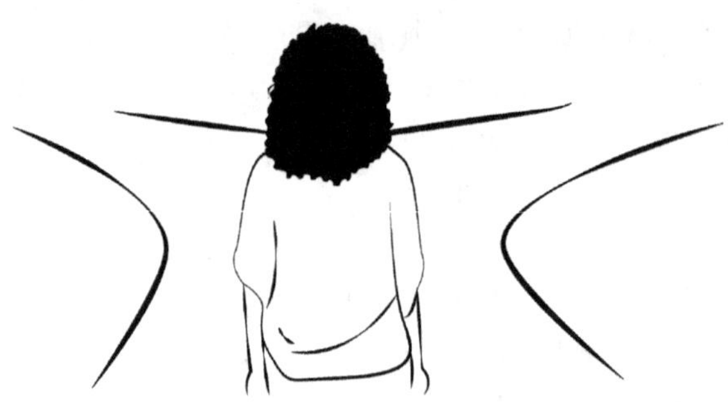

COME INSIDE

Come inside and experience my love
it's warm, it's peaceful, it's magical
you will be safe in my arms in my love
you won't have to run or hide
no ego or pride resides in my love
my love is patient and understanding
it's forgiving and not demanding
come inside and be loved
come inside and be free
come inside and let me love you, all of you
come inside and be with me

THE MAN I WANT

I want a man who plans dates
calls more than he texts
who wants more than sex
a connection, offering protection and affection

I want a man who seeks to know me
not mold me or scold me
but speaks to me with kindness in his voice
he knows I'm the best choice
for his heart, his mind, his soul
a man not afraid to take control

I want a man who is not afraid to love me
who will pray for me and teach me
who is not intimidated by me
who will make me a better woman
and in turn I will make him a better man
who will do whatever he can
to make sure I understand
that I am the only woman he desires

I want a man with integrity and honesty
who will take care of my heart

and not rip it apart
who loves me unconditionally, respectfully, and carefully
in private and in public
because he is proud to walk alongside me

I want a man who wants me
who I don't have to chase
compete or race
with other females
I want a man sent by God
who is not a fraud
who knows who he is
and gives
all the love he has inside
and sets aside his pride
who will make me his bride
but most importantly...love me

19

THE SUN AND THE RAIN

When the sun shines

There is this happiness inside

A feeling of warmth

A feeling of joy

A feeling of optimism

Your spirits are lifted

Your mood has shifted

Then all of a sudden it rains

When the rain comes

We feel at peace

Our soul is cleansed

We may feel sad

We may feel relieved

We may even be confused

But in order to have the sun you need the rain

To wash away the pain

life is full of sun and rain

hope and pain

love and loss

choices and chances

mistakes and opportunities

happiness and sadness

so appreciate the rain

because without it there is no sun

DREAMING

I am dreaming
thinking and waiting
hoping and praying
anticipating
wishing and missing
YOU.

GOD SAID

God said

be patient, your time is coming

God said

have faith, don't worry

God said

trust in me and I won't fail you

God said

I got you

trust me

pray to me

lean on me

God said

you got this

you are strong

you are powerful

you can do all things

because of me

God said

I'll never leave you

God said

I believe in you

God said I am with you

God said

just breathe
be still
and know that I am God

I LOVE YOU DEEP

I love you deep

deep down in my soul

our love will never grow old

your love flows deep like a river

it makes my soul quiver

your love runs deep like the ocean

it's like a magic potion

a drug that I can never get enough of

Your love is suffocating, yet intoxicating

It's mesmerizing and sometimes surprising

It's uplifting and inspirational

encouraging and motivational

a deep love I have been longing for

waiting and praying for

God knew I couldn't wait any more

So he sent me a deep, everlasting love.

SON

God gave me a son
Who is my pride and joy
An amazing little boy
that loves me
And will cherish me to eternity
who brings out the best in me
He teaches me patience and understanding
He makes me a better person
A better woman
He is my heart
The greatest gift I never knew I needed
He is my one and only son

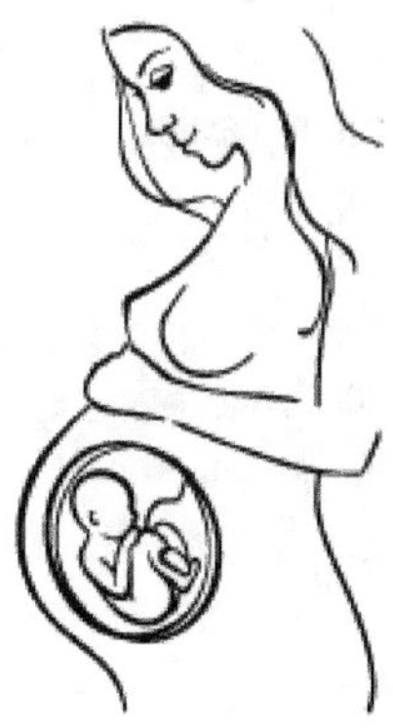

BLESSINGS

You ever just sit back and count your blessings
and think of all the lessons
that got you where you are today
there's no way
you would have made it thus far
without the man above
who has shown you so much love

You ever just sit back and wonder
and ponder
about the choices you've made
all of the shade
that comes your way because you are blessed
not stressed
and worried about what the next person got
you keep your head held high
to the sky and wave bye
to all the hating and negativity
you push through with positivity
and make it to your destination
without hesitation
using your motivation
from within

ain't it a sin
that some folks would rather hate on you
because they ain't you
but you don't worry about them
you stand tall
and let them fall
while you are counting your blessings

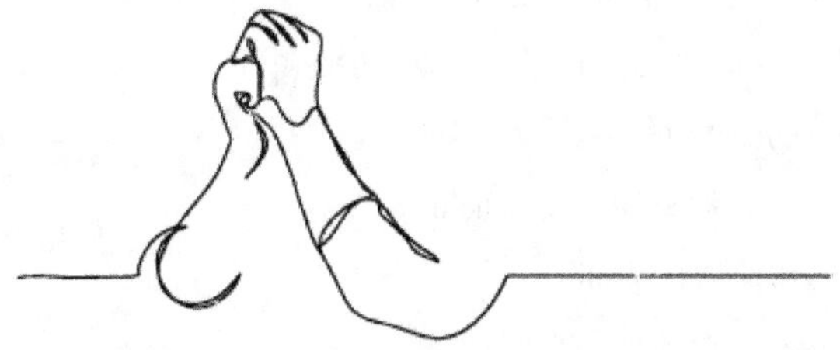

HATE IN OUR HEARTS

They say home is where the heart is

And our hearts should be filled with love

Then somebody explain to me why there's so much

hate in our hearts, our lives, our worlds

Why do we think with our hearts instead of our heads

Make the wrong decision and end up dead

Alone, out in the street with nothing to eat

No one to look up to and nothing to believe in

Except our sins,

when we know there is something

we really care about

Yeah, we get angry but why fight

When we can scream and shout

Why kill when you can just chill

And be happy that you're alive

And able to strive for that goal

That is the key to your future

Why don't we stop to think

Before we take that drink

that's gonna take us over the edge

why can't we appreciate what we have

instead of worrying about what we don't

and smoking that joint

how can home be where the heart is

when our hearts are black as coal

and folks still sell their soul

just to make it

because they can't take it no more

tired of being broke

don't take your life for a joke

tired of being mad and sad

do something that will make you happy and glad

tired of people bringing you down

find some new friends to hang around

you ain't gotta get down

with the crazy stuff that other folks do

your heart ain't gotta be filled with hate

don't you know that you change your fate

your mind ain't gotta be full of negative things

think positive about life and the joy it can bring

your life can be what you want it to be

open your eyes to see

that peace and love are what we need

to strive and succeed

take the hate out of your heart

make a fresh start

we are so far apart

from where we should be

you hold the key
to life, liberty and the pursuit of happiness
so get all that hate up out yo chest
put it to rest
may god bless
and restore PEACE to our world

THE POWER WITHIN

You have the power within to achieve your goals

Don't let anybody put your dreams on hold

You have the power within to do what's right

Stand up for what you believe in put up a good fight

You have the power within to be the best

There will always be difficulties cause life is one big test

That you can not fail

That you can not redo

That you can not get back once it's gone

And all the wrong

You've done cannot be erased

And you're left with a stupid look on your face

Cause you forgot to embrace

Your power within

MY FAITH HAS BEEN TESTED

My faith has been tested
there have been times when I've wanted to give up
but I kept going
never knowing
if I was going to reach my destination
God sometimes tests us to see how much faith we have
how patient we can be
how much we believe in him
our faith is often tested
 right when we are about to give up
then all of a sudden there is a breakthrough
a miracle, a testimony
you don't even know how you got there
you are surprised at the outcome
it's wasn't what you did, or what you said
but rather God's grace and mercy
you passed the test and life goes on
until your faith is tested again
but this time you are prepared
you can handle it
because you believe
and know that God will see you through